D&M Between 2 Men

Also by Andrew Drake and published by Ginninderra Press
Beauty in the Darkness
Limerick Lovers (with Jill Wherry) (Picaro Poets)

Also by Martin Christmas and published by Ginninderra Press
Immediate Reflections (Picaro Poets)
The Deeper Inner (Pocket Poets)

Andrew Drake
&
Martin Christmas

D&M Between 2 Men

D & M Between 2 Men
ISBN 978 1 76041 777 2
Copyright © text Andrew Drake and Martin Christmas 2019
Cover photo: Martin Christmas

First published 2019 by
GINNINDERRA PRESS
PO Box 3461 Port Adelaide 5015 Australia
www.ginninderrapress.com.au

Contents

D&Ms	Andrew	7
Secret men's business	Martin	8
Words	Andrew	10
Man up	Martin	11
Mansplaining 101	Andrew	12
Women are never wrong	Martin	14
Man	Martin	16
The Earth is a woman	Andrew	17
The role of women	Martin	18
Equity	Andrew	19
Miss and Mister	Andrew	20
Love is	Andrew	21
Love	Martin	23
Plainspeak	Martin	24
Sometimes	Andrew	26
Switching off	Andrew	27
Aloneness	Martin	29
Insecure distress	Martin	31
Consequences	Martin	33
Nightmares	Andrew	35
Return Nightmares	Martin	37
Kasplat	Andrew	38
Boys do cry	Andrew	40
Tears & Fears & Feelings	Martin	42
Fathers and Sons	Martin	44
Not a perfect dad	Andrew	46
Empowerment	Martin	48
Violence	Andrew	49
Abuse	Andrew	50
Buzz Aldrin	Andrew	52

Masculine and Feminine	Martin	55
Three wise monkeys	Andrew	57
Man angst	Martin	59
Masculinity	Martin	60
End poem	Andrew & Martin	62

D&Ms

Men can talk about anything,
unless it's anything personal because
they don't usually have heart to hearts.

And they don't always think with their brains,
in fact, the first time a lady asked me
for a D&M I thought it was a kink
and apparently it was, because
there was nothing conventional to me
about discussing my personal life.

Remember, guys don't cry.
They are masculine,
unless they have the man flu
which doesn't make them feminine.

Women are feminine
and they can go through childbirth,
yet men can't go through a common cold
because they're only strong physically.

Mentally, men are weak,
ready to shatter at any given moment,
because they believe that
deep and meaningfuls
are shallow and meaningless,
as they were never taught the basics
of how to let everything out.

Andrew

Secret men's business

Hey bro, you can't say
that shit, or write it,
that's secret men's biz.
The lads will think
we're weak, effeminate,
even have feelings.

The ladies will think
we're little boys who
need a lesson or 2
in manning up.

Man –
that's the key word.

Bro, you've opened
up a can of worms, a
real Pandora's Box.
Soon we'll be sharing
words like feelings,
insecurity, fears
and tears.

Who knows
where it will end?
The little boy within
is whispering in my ear,
'If only we could get
away with it.'

Man hug coming your
way. Never said it,
never wrote it,
would sound too g—.

Martin

Words

Words hold power
but the world changes
with or without them.
If we exile our speech
we'll be left speechless
and if we wear insults like a badge
they will wear us out.
So we, as a society,
manipulate our vocabulary
to rebel against a dictionary
until the day the majority say it isn't OK
for us to utter the word gay;
happiness rebranded as an insult,
with homosexuals caught in between.

Words hold power.
Men hold men.
Definitions are endless.
The world will continue to change.

Andrew

Man up

Just words –
Gay
Straight
Trans
Manspeak
Mansplaining
Banter
Tears
Fears
Feelings
Loneliness
Fathers
Sons
Nightmares
Stereotypes
Violence
Abuse
Truth
Empowerment –
Just words.
Man up.
It's OK.
Speak up.
Be heard!

Martin

Mansplaining 101

I understand women.

When a woman says, 'I'm fine'
she is not fine.
It probably means she's hungry,
and she doesn't belong in the kitchen,
so offer to cook her some food.
She most likely wants a coffee too,
make one just in case.

If this doesn't work,
apologise.
You must've done something wrong,
perhaps in her dream,
also mention your assumption
that it must have been in her dream.

If she is still upset,
you should ask her again.
The more you ask
the more it will show that you care.
Afterwards, accuse her of lying,
she wasn't fine and you caught her out
on a lie.
This will show her that honesty
is important to you.

Then bring up other women
who have claimed that they were fine.
Go into detail,
make comparisons
because women love facts.
This demonstrates your high level
of knowledge and expertise,
and there's nothing sexier to a woman
than proving her wrong.

Follow this up by asking her
if it's that time of the month,
she will appreciate that you remembered.
Then set a reminder and mention it
every month from then on.

And if all else fails
tell her to calm down.
This will calm her,
helping her to realise
that she was just being over dramatic.
She will love your straightforwardness
and will agree that it really wasn't
important at all.

And when a man says, 'I'm fine'
he is most likely fine.

Andrew

Women are never wrong

Noooooooo bro, you've gone too far,
you'll be shot down with this attack,
even tongue in cheek.
The little lady shouldn't see your missile,
red alert, not false alarm.
The real deal. Protect ya balls.
Never underestimate the power of a chick,
they seldom get it wrong, in their head that is.
Ya gotta learn to play along and read the wind,
don't call the shots or ya dead meat for sure.
I once had a bird, damn fine she was,
taken by her hook, line, you know the drill.
We were together for quite a time, she was an
OK good woman, in my eyes anyway.
She had one small flaw.
When she rang I said, 'Hello?'
Her line, 'Let's meet up. A little chat.'
Lasted 3 hours long and all
my faults revealed.
A little manboy
being whacked by 'mum' for sure,
until I knew
I was being used as bait,
and stopped it when her parents
visited and we were in the act
and she called out, 'I'll be done soon,
just wait in the other room'
and my best part shrank down,
it wasn't even winter!

The deed was done.
The man? He fled.
Dead man running.

Was with Dan on Granite Island
a few years later and saw her
with her new beau. I said to Dan,
'Run and hide.' Be wise in time.
The power of a woman
must never be denied.

Martin

Man

What's it like to be a man?
Is that light or dark skinned?
Muslim, Christian, atheist or other?
Oldest, youngest or only child?
Tall, short, fat or thin?
Fit or not?
Artist or nine-to-fiver?
Pacifist or warmonger?
Aussie or Afghan?
Rich or poor?
You or me?

Ask me when I'm older.
I'll have an answer (maybe not).
Till then it's hypothetical.

What's a woman?

Martin

The Earth is a woman

I've heard the Earth is a woman
and I realised that our population
is fighting about whether the world
is flat or curvy,
the same way people fight
against whether women
should be flat or curvy.
Every argument is to disprove
the legitimacy of the other
rather than accept that we
see the world differently.

I see a beautiful
life giving world
filled with wonder.

In truth,
if we focused less with our eyes
and more with our hearts,
we would find that her shape
has no boundaries.
For she isn't defined by her design,
she is so much more.

Andrew

The role of women

Blonde, brunette, whatever,
their spirit cannot be denied.

A reference point regardless,
integral to the fostering of life.

Whether
mother
sister
wife.

This little verse is not a sop
but a homage to equality.

Don't get me wrong,
both of us are strong.

We are their equals, they of us
2 parts of the same equation.

Let it always be thus.

Martin

Equity

Men and women go to great lengths
to measure up,
but a ruler is not a measuring tape.
We are blurred, straight, curled lines
circling around the block;
a flatlined pulse
on her rollercoaster,
heading from A to Z
alphabetically
while she travels
chronologically.

We are equal,
but we are different pieces
to the same puzzle,
inclusively exclusive,
disabled by our contrast
in nature and nurture
because men and women
are untranslatable,
unsolved mysteries
to each other.

For the greatest riddle
is the truth
that we never say.

Andrew

Miss and Mister

When a Miss and a Mister become friends
they often misinterpret the situation
by misconstruing and misunderstanding
the misleading signs.
These miscalculations involving
this mismatched friendship
can cause misconceptions where
one ends up misjudging these engagements
which leads to misdeveloped feelings
of being mistreated.
They see the other as misbehaving
through misdirection rather than
it just being a misperception.

Whether they were misinformed,
misguided, or misrepresented
is misfortunate, but it ends up
creating mistrust between the two
based upon basic miscommunication
until they are both miserable.
And I wonder,
'What are we missing?'

Andrew

Love is

Love isn't a cliché,
it makes no sense
and it doesn't come easy.
Love is rare,
it has no rhyme or reason
and it isn't perfect.
It's every flaw in between.

Love is holding your heart
because it physically aches too much.
Love is waking up at 4 a.m.
and immediately spreading your arms out,
searching the bed for her
before realising that you slept alone.
Love is every near miss
and each moment
where she was just out of reach.

Love is when every single thing
in this whole world reminds you of her.
Love is a lifelong addiction
that never leaves your mind.
Love is knowing that you are only half
of your true self,
believing that your other half is out there
searching for you.

Love is when you see all of these dangers
and yet you are still willing to risk
your entire life and all of yourself,
as even just one chance
at a single moment with her is worth it,
because you know
that there is no life without her.

Andrew

Love

Love is a complex word.
Love is not just about Love.

Love, ancient concept, biblical even.
Didn't Jesus express it many times?

Cain and Abel. Prodigal son stuff.
Love versus Hate. All you need is Love.

Always Love, not Hate. Time is short.
Too short to Hate. Love is a full time job.

Old English, German, Scandinavian, Latin
leof, luba, lof, lubet...pleasing, desire, dear.

Over used? Love. 4 letters meaning much.
Love, not Hate.

I Love peanut paste.
I Love sunrises and sunsets.
I Love the equation 1 plus 1 equals bliss.
I LOVE…LIFE.

Love is all around.

Martin

Plainspeak

Not easy
for a man to say
what he means and
mean what he says.
He's always second guessing
how it will be taken
by you know who.

There is a gulf between men
and women's
plainspeak for sure.

Let me explain.

The thing between my legs is a penis.
It doesn't make me a dickhead.
The thing between her legs is a vagina.
It doesn't make her a c—t.
We both have nipples and a belly button.
She gives birth, but I am part of
the life creation process,
unless she used IVF.

I'm a man, not a little boy.
She's a woman, not a little toy.
Being a midlife man who likes kids
doesn't make me a paedophile.

Words such as
homophobia and misogyny
are negotiated through
intricate and subtle concepts.
But sexism is what it is –
see it for what it is.
Man or woman, makes no diff.

Manspeak, womenspeak, plainspeak.
Trying to be fluent in each
is no easy task.

Martin

Sometimes

Sometimes, I feel like I'm having
silent conversations with myself
between the cryptic sentences
I string together for everyone else.
Ambiguous yet chivalrous,
a gentleman, opening the door
to his mind for you,
subtly laying out all the pieces
to his future.
However, the order is jumbled,
not every piece fits,
and the ones that do are missing.

Sometimes, I feel like
my silent conversations
are so loud that I can barely
string sentences together.

Sometimes, I wish that you could solve
all of my mysteries.

Sometimes, I need to help you help me.

Andrew

Switching off

If my body is a temple
then my heart and soul
light these sacred halls,
and though I'm not short fused,
when my wires get crossed
my power goes out
and my sanctuary gets dark.

I switch off because I refuse
to believe that I can't
brighten this whole world,
and through this I end up
paralysed inside,
by my own volition.

It's internally exhausting
and emotionally overwhelming
to accept that I have limitations
that create relentless reservations
as to why I push away
when others try to light the way.

And when my body
doesn't feel like a temple,
I still have people
who pray for me
to the powers that be
regardless of what I believe,
with others who unequivocally
choose to sit in the dark with me.

They all see me depleted,
looking defeated,
and while some have retreated,
many proceeded
to accept me
in my darkest hours.

I'm starting to realise
that we are all at our best
at any given day,
but there are some moments
that are darker than others.
And I'm beginning to learn
that in those times,
when we refuse to open up,
we end up shutting down.

Andrew

Aloneness

Women talk glass ceilings.
I talk about glass walls, wondering
if other men feel emptiness,
aloneness.
However hard you try to
be accepted, you just
fall short of expectations.
Isn't everyone having a ball
surrounded by others 24/7,
living the dream, while I,
home,
alone.

I wonder, are they really
as happy as they make out,
or is it all a front, an affront.
Are they just as isolated,
even in a room of others,
and I in my room alone
but seldom lonely.
I'm rambling now.

Mirrored hallway.
The only reflection is your own.
Is there anybody out there?

Pause to think.

I've known nothing else since
just a boy in my own world
for one reason or another.
The boy became a man.
The glass wall grew as well.
Am I happy? Sure,
until I know I'm not.

Martin

Insecure distress

I am torn between wanting to hold on to
or moving forward to
whatever waits around the bend,
to leap out of the darkness
or shine a light onto
what's been writ.

Hamlet knew he wasn't mad.
What if he really did express
his insecure distress,
or exploded with self doubt,
or he'd lashed out, or thrown
a coward's punch, or worse?

Am I the only man not always sure,
feeling distress which can't be seen,
or neat expressed, and hides
it from the world or loved one near,
and become a half man?
Women seem to do it well,
why can't we as men
be bravely insecure?

Lightning's stunning flash
lights up the void. Distress.

Do you have nightmares? So do I.
Like a boy-man, and tears sometimes.
and no amount of being told, 'Man up'
can stop the flow, and then I think,
Pandora's Box, and while there's life
there's hope, and breathe, and move
again along a positivity path
towards the Light and not the
Dark.

To be brave and strong.
To speak up.
Which is the question?
Which is the answer?

Martin

Consequences

I once knew this young buck
who had no external fear.
Steadfast. Inner strength.
Outer resolve. Hardships lifelong.
Respected him for his daily courage.
Great smile and great laugh.
Even though I taunted him
verbally, pulled his beard,
(could have been a Viking, pale skin but
very strong), and crossed the line
by putting a knife to his throat,
(not a Croc Dundee
but a small blunt kitchen knife),
and mocked him more in
banter, alpha male way.
He sprang like a tiger fierce,
and if for real, I would have died.
I stepped back fast. Defeated.

He just smiled back and
said he knew it was in jest and
knew the consequences.
He winked like the warrior he was,
then added, 'But if you hurt
the one I truly love, I'd
damage you beyond repair.
You'd know the consequences
of your action, the pain
prolonged, would be intense,
you wouldn't smile but know that all
men have a darker side which we
control – most times – excepting
in our resting nightmares.'

Martin

Nightmares

I have worse experiences in my head
when I have nightmares
than I do, out in the real world,
because you can't outrun
your inner demons.
And when you fight yourself,
you're always going to end up getting hurt
beating yourself up over false realities.

I have died countless times.

I've been killed and I've killed myself
but the nightmares always roll on.
I've seen things in my nightmares
that to this day haven't left me.
I can still picture two familiar eyeballs
melting like sun-dried tomatoes in summer.

Images like these are burnt into my brain,
and they may not be real,
but the sweats and the screams are,
the tears and the anxiety I feel are,
and they stay with me
long after I wake up.

I don't want to feel this any more.

I want to dream the way I hear
dreams are supposed to be,
but dreams are what I have
while I'm awake,
so I'll stay awake,
and I won't rest until
all of my dreams come true.

Andrew

Return Nightmares

Hey buddy,
I'm a grown man
but still frightened
like a little boy.

Nightmares.
Powerful shit
when we are
most alone.

It's dark.
I'm running from
another man. Scared.
Side streets. Back gardens.
Brick walls.
Over fences. Hiding.
Still he pursues me.
Why?

Nightmares.
Still a little boy at heart.
I want my mummy!

And then, release of sorts.
Something deep inside
says, 'Face your fears.'
I stop running. Wake up.
He's gone. Daytime.
Will he return tonight?

Why did I never cry for help?

Martin

Kasplat

I remember this one good day with my mum
between desertions.
I had just turned 8 and she bought me a toy dog
wearing a Christmas hat.
Straight away I began lifting him up by his hat.
I was so happy.
Kasplat he'd go, as he fell back to reality
where he curiously listened to my mother
as she yelled incoherently in the background.

I yanked his hat harder, and higher he went.
I was so happy.
Kasplat he'd go, as he came crashing down
where he witnessed the side effects
of a drug addiction that had gone on
for too long.

I yanked his hat faster and faster
as I zoomed around the room.
I was so happy.

Kasplat.
                Kasplat.
                                Kasplat,
as the threads of his hat began to break
while he felt the pure joy of a child receiving
their first and last gift from their mum.

I sat with Kasplat next to the fireplace
and I held him tightly.
I was so happy
as he sniffed the air filled with
second-hand smoke and fire
as his fur set alight.

I spent the whole night picking off burnt fabric.
I was so happy
when I knew that he wasn't broken,
just a little less furry.
I took him home
and he never left me
as he travelled from house to house to shed
where he ended up in a red plastic box.
Years passed until just last week
when I remembered Kasplat,
and went into the shed
to find him
and play with him
again and again and again.

                                    Kasplat.

                Kasplat.

Kasplat.

He was so happy.

Andrew

Boys do cry

There was a time when I couldn't cry.

I was 14 years old and it lasted a year
until finally I cried for a day straight.
I still remember where I was,
who was with me,
and what the catalyst was.
The boy who found me sobbing
was the school bully.
He showed me humanity.

But it didn't prevent me from having
another year's drought between tears,
and in that time I heard terms like:
Boys don't cry.
Be masculine.
Man up.

But I'll tell you this,
I cried
While watching the movie *Titanic*.
When reminiscing over bad memories.
While having the flu.
When missing someone,
feeling overwhelmed and helpless.

Sometimes I cry for no reason.

Crying doesn't affect my manhood:
I have a beard,
but I'm no more of a man.
I can barely change a tyre,
but I'm no less of a man.

We can be courageous and sensitive,
for tears have nothing to do with gender.

I am a man because I say I am,
nothing more,
nothing less.

Andrew

Tears & Fears & Feelings

Tears & Fears & Cobber.
Dad said, 'Be a man.' I was only 8.
I still tear up when thinking of my
beautiful dog, my first true friend.
I still tear up, even as a now grown
man. What's wrong
with feelings?

12 years after my mum died,
I'm driving down the coast.
Mum loved the sea.
Suddenly I tear up
and bawl my eyes out
at her memory.
Was necessary.
Tears & Fears & Feelings.

20 years or so ago,
a young mate hanged himself
from a beam in his parent's ceiling.
Always smiling, Joe never
showed his inner feelings.
The note to his mum and dad
ended with, 'I love you.'
Too late to unman up.
20 years on, his suicide still hurts.
These days I ask R U OK?
and listen sensitively.
Too late for Joe, but might help
others break through their outer
silence and seek help.

My father was a stoic man,
I never saw him cry or show
emotion when I was growing up,
so no close male adult
to teach the Tears & Fears &
Feelings thing.
He only hugged me once,
'Love you, son.'
I replied, 'You'll crack a rib.'
With hindsight, a better answer
would have done the trick. Too
late, he died the next year after.
Tears & Fears & Feelings.
Real men understand
their purpose.

Martin

Fathers and Sons

My father was a
gentle man, but
stiff upper lip
and all that.
A free spirit
whose overbearing father
forced him to the Middle East
when he was 22. He lived
the life of Lawrence
of Arabia. Toughened him
up mightily, impervious
to pain.

When he had his first born son –
me – he wouldn't guide him
towards being a sensitive,
caring, loving man,
but just a life-long boy
under his life-long spell.

I am still that boy
in many ways.
Not easy in the company
of other men. Afraid,
even as boys can be.
Only now, learning to banter
with other men, being unafraid
to cross the boundaries,
to push and shove,
hug and love. Happy to
understand my role.

To those who have sons.
Play the Dad
and not the strict and hurtful
Father. Your boy
will grow to be a
man, a real man,
not a bully gentleman.

Martin

Not a perfect dad

I was 13 years old when I realised
my dad wasn't perfect.
I always knew it about my mum
but my dad was different.
He was my light before I knew
how dark my world was,
and before I knew
how dark his world had been.

As a child, I saw my dad as
the smartest,
the strongest,
and the funniest.
He was brave, with the biggest heart.
The world's greatest Dad,
as it said on his mug.
The same mug nearly every Dad gets.

He was the kind of Dad
that changed all my nappies,
spoon fed me my meals
and read me stories.
Nothing taught me mortality
more than the moment
I began doing these things for my dad…

My son is now 13 years old.
I'm scared.
I think he's realising
that I'm not perfect either,
but if I read this to him
he'd probably tell me not to worry
because he knew that years ago
and that he loves me all the same.

When people tell me I'm a good dad,
I reply that my son is the amazing one.
He's my light after I knew
how dark my world was,
and I'm just lucky,
but I will not be returning
my world's greatest Dad mug
any time soon.

Andrew

Empowerment

(In my imagination, for I have no son).

Son (I hesitate).

Yes, dad?

Time for a man to man chat
(a real Pandora's Box):
Men & Women.
Dreams & Nightmares.
Inner & Outer.
Stereotypes & Prejudices.
Truth.

Struth, dad, a can of worms.

Yeah, mate (bonding).
let's go for a drive.
Maybe Victor Harbor.
Here are the keys.
You drive.

Love you, dad!

Thanks, son.
Glad we had this little chat
between us men.
(What has been done?)

Martin

Violence

I was sitting with my dad in the lounge, watching his favourite show, when an advert appeared. 'Violence against women, Australia says no.' So I asked him, 'If Australia said no, why do we need an ad?' And he turns to me, looking sad and says, 'A long time ago I was watching TV, just like this, when an advert appeared, showing a girl in a bikini. This was completely unplanned. Your mum walked in and then stabbed a screwdriver right through my hand.' I'm not one to be speechless, but I didn't know what I could have said, so I asked, 'Was it a Phillips head or a flat head?' We spent the next few minutes looking at the scar, trying to figure it out while I was processing what it was all about. I'd like to imagine that he screamed, 'Jesus Christ', as his hand was holier than thou, crucified. He was stuck and hurt and all I was thinking was, 'Where was my dad's advert?' He said, 'Violence is wrong, no matter the gender you were born', and this he proved with all the scars he has worn, while trying so damn hard to stay strong. We switched off the TV that day and he cried for so long because, even though, with violence against women, thank God Australia says no. When it comes to violence against men, Australia says nothing.

Andrew

Abuse

I know what abuse feels like,
I've suffered all forms and variations,
silently.
It was normal life to me
feeling helpless and numb,
desensitised but I survived.
My greatest fear became
the inability to feel afraid
and humour was the instrument
to help me through the pain,
so I lost my filter and made jokes
about the world that broke me down
and many times I went too far.

I wish it wasn't too late
to confess to the people I've hurt,
'My goal was to make you smile with me,
laugh with me,
laugh at me.
But please don't cry because of me.'
Maybe things would have been different
if you all knew that I went through it too.
If I could, I would go back
into the past,
not to take back what I said
or to justify my actions,
but to tell each of them I'm sorry
before it became too late.

I am so very sorry.
I want us to scream that we survived
while I help carry every sadness.
Then we can all cry together
silently.
But I can't because
we didn't all survive.

Andrew

Buzz Aldrin

Growing up,
if I said that I was the forgotten child
it would be putting it mildly,
as while my brothers acted wildly,
I was considered normal.
And it was normal for me when they hurt me.
It was normal for me to be abused.
It was normal for me to cry myself to sleep,
broken and confused,
realising that it wasn't normal.

I love seeing happy families
because I wouldn't want my upbringing
to be the measure of success,
because it's not my measure.
I am a believer
in never stopping, because neither
your past or your present should stop you
from the future you've always wanted.
And my normality taught me
that I wanted to be special.

And every time I tried so hard
I always fell just short,
as I was never taught
that it's possible to seek support.
My brain found ways to make fun of me,
dubbing me Buzz Aldrin,
the second man on the moon.
Always number two.
So when you see me celebrating,
it's not egotistical.
The moon is just very far away
and I was brought up
being taught that I would never make it.
And I'm beginning to realise
that it's not so bad
to reach the moon second,
when I didn't have a rocket
or a spacesuit
or a map.

I'm still learning how to be like the children
who grew up in those happy families,
but you can only learn so much
from a distance.
And I was like a helium balloon
that no one wanted to hold on to.
So now I feel stuck on the moon.
Maybe I tried too hard, too soon,
and perhaps I should appreciate
that the most beautiful places
are isolated and uninhabited,
but I just don't want to be
forgotten any more.

I heard it only takes 42 folds
of a piece of paper
to reach the moon,
so I'll fold up this poem
and hope that it reaches you.

Andrew

Masculine and Feminine

During this quest to discover who I am,
a revelation catches by surprise in a cafe
while talking to a woman about a poem
I wanted her to read.

The role of bad cop to my frightened male.
She's having difficulties and I'm wondering why.
Seems simple as a guy, I have no qualms.
She says, 'I've always played the victim,
this is tough going. I am not tough'.

We reach a mutual agreement on how
to play 'the role' and shared a few life
experiences. She then plays the part
as if she were a tough cop all her life.
I wonder at this moment,
'How many times we victim-play.'

We then talk secret human business,
not masculine or feminine but real shit.
The gap between us disappears as we reveal
more similarities than differences.
We hug and in this moment, I understand.

We go our separate ways refreshed.
Mansplaining. Womensplaining. People explaining.
One to one as two adults life changed.
Homo sapiens both on their separate journeys.
The quest goes on for both of us.

One has a penis, the other a vagina.
An easy fit, you'd think.

Martin

Three wise monkeys

We are not flawless or perfect
but neither are we ignorant,
for you and I are more similar
than we are different.
My eyes are not your eyes
and yet we both can see.
My ears are not your ears
and yet we both can listen.
My lips are not your lips
and yet we both can speak.
Because we've both seen evil,
we have both heard evil,
and we have both spoken evil,
but it doesn't make us evil.

My heart is not your heart
and yet we both can love.
My fears are not your fears
and yet we both are scared sometimes.
My strengths are not your strengths
and my struggles are not your struggles
and yet we can be strong together
and we can cry together,
because we have both seen good,
we have both heard good,
and we have both spoken good,
but it doesn't make us good.

We are not flawless or perfect,
neither good or evil.
We balance on a shifting line
and sometimes we fall the wrong way,
because when inundated with choices,
we won't choose wisely everyday.
But each decision that we've made
led us to this exact moment,
and every step we took
brought us to this choice.
For my home is not your home
and yet if you knock,
I will always open the door.
It will never be too late,
because you never have to be alone.

Andrew

Man angst

Is it too big
or too small
to do the job?
You know what I mean.

How do I stack up
beside the other guys?

Will she think I'm queer
if I tear up during
a movie or make a
sensitive comment on
what she's wearing?
Does it make a man more
loveable, huggable?

Man angst – is it always so?
No.

Feeding breadcrumbs
to an injured pigeon.
Nursing a small baby,
so.

Being with the one
you truly love.
Waking in the morning with
them beside you.
Sweet chariot swing
low.

Martin

Masculinity

More than appears at first glance.

Two men
sitting on a back porch couch
one bloody hot afternoon.

The talk –
mothers, fathers,
sons, brothers,
sensitive, brutal,
strong, masculine,
intimate, manangst,
past, present, future.
But who knows when the bell tolls
and for whom?

Sadness, regret,
gladness, acceptance.

Masculine. Feminine.
The two go hand in hand
to make a male complete.

Two hours flash by.
Both have had their fill.
Walk up the street
to the visitor's car.
Some banter. Laughter.
Final embrace.
Male friendship –
a safe place for both.

Masculinity.

More than appears at first glance.

Martin

End poem

Martin	Maybe we should turn this D&M
Between 2 Men
into a poetry book?
Andrew	That's a terrible idea!
I would appreciate it
if you deleted this whole
conversation.
Martin	Sure.
Will do.
Trust me.
Just a D&M Between 2 men.
How many 'n's in Ginninderra?

Andrew & Martin

Andrew Drake

Andrew Drake is an established written and spoken word poet from South Australia. He was the 2017 South Australian Poetry Slam Champion and a four-time state finalist. Andrew has found success in countless competitions, including winning at the Adelaide Fringe Festival three times; winning the Yankalilla Poetry Slam in 2019; coming runner-up in the Goolwa Poetry Cup; and at the Singapore Poetry Slam. He was the featured poet in Singapore, in Bali, and around Australia, and has also performed in the Sydney Opera House. Andrew has run poetry workshops in Australia and in Bali. In 2017, he co-wrote a chapbook with Jill Wherry called *Limerick Lovers*, and in 2019, his first full-length collection of poetry, *Beauty in the Darkness*, was published by Ginninderra Press.

Martin Christmas

Martin Christmas lives in Adelaide, South Australia; has a Master of Arts in Australian Cultural Studies; and is a poet, photographer and trained theatre director. He has been published in several Australian anthologies, including Friendly Street Poets and *Tamba* and overseas, including *Red River Review* (USA) (as a featured poet); *Illya's Honey* (USA); and *StepAway Magazine* (UK). He runs community poetry presentation workshops and teaches presentation elements to young poets. He has been published by Ginninderra Press (*Immediate Reflections* and *The Deeper Inner*). His first full-length poetry book of poems and photographs, *Random Adventures*, will be published by Ginninderra Press in late 2019. His poetic eye often focuses on the small or the seemingly mundane, revealing underneath truths. A lifelong theatre background has become a great asset in the way he visualises the written word.

www.ingramcontent.com/pod-product-compliance
Lightning Source LLC
Chambersburg PA
CBHW062200100526
44589CB00014B/1881